T0273107

Intergenerational Transfers under Community Rating

Intergenerational Transfers under Community Rating

David F. Bradford and
Derrick A. Max

The AEI Press

Publisher for the American Enterprise Institute

WASHINGTON, D.C.

1996

The authors would like to thank Sherry Glied, Jagadeesh Gokhale, Laurence Kotlikoff, Gregory Spencer, Carolyn Weaver, and members of the Health Economics Group of the National Bureau of Economic Research for comments and assistance with data. Ryan Edwards provided exceptionally skillful research assistance. David Bradford's work on transition incidence has benefited from the financial support of the John M. Olin Foundation. Views expressed are those of the authors and should not be taken as representing any other people or institutions.

Distributed to the Trade by National Book Network, 15200 NBN Way, Blue Ridge Summit, PA 17214. To order call toll free 1-800-462-6420 or 1-717-794-3800. For all other inquiries please contact the AEI Press, 1150 Seventeenth Street, N.W., Washington, D.C. 20036 or call 1-800-862-5801.

ISBN 0-8447-7033-7
ISBN 978-0-8447-7033-8
1   3   5   7   9   10   8   6   4   2

q 1996 by the American Enterprise Institute for Public Policy Research, Washington, D.C. All rights reserved. No part of this publication may be used or reproduced in any manner whatsoever without permission in writing from the American Enterprise Institute except in the case of brief quotations embodied in news articles, critical articles, or reviews. The views expressed in the publications of the American Enterprise Institute are those of the authors and do not necessarily reflect the views of the staff, advisory panels, officers, or trustees of AEI.

THE AEI PRESS
Publisher for the American Enterprise Institute
1150 17th Street, N.W., Washington, D.C. 20036

Contents

I t is widely understood that government can accomplish through regulation many of the same objectives as are served by expenditure programs. A typical regulatory mandate—for example, a requirement that local governments ensure the attainment of some specified level of drinking water purity—can be equated with a combination of an expenditure program (compensation for the cost of attaining the specified water quality) and a tax program (a tax on communities whose water quality falls short of the target standard). Observers have often suggested that it would serve consistent public policy to bring such regulatory decisions into the same budgetary framework as applies to spending and taxing. Absent such an innovation, some would take comfort in the belief that, since a regulatory program perforce carries within itself its own financing, it cannot alter the budget deficit.

If, however, one regards a budget deficit as an indicator of a transfer of fiscal burdens toward younger and future generations, the comfort would be misplaced. This volume concerns an important example of a regulatory program that has been seriously considered without, apparently, any recognition that its economic effect would be a very significant transfer of fiscal burdens toward the young and unborn. The example is a mandated purchase of (or provision by employers of) health care insurance under a system of community rating.

Advocates of health care reform legislation have various goals, which we may divide in the usual economists' way into distributional and allocational objectives. Among the allocational objectives would be the goal of correcting perceived or actual defects in the functioning of the market for health care and, especially, for health insurance (more precisely, insurance against the event of having a demand for certain health care services). Into this category would go the objective of controlling health care costs. Here the imperfections to be corrected are often created by existing policy interventions, especially the favorable income tax treatment of health care expenditures covered by employers, as well as various regulatory constraints (such as mandates requiring that particular services be covered in allowable insurance policies). In addition, many believe that adverse selection gives rise to excessive commitment of resources to underwriting and presents an opportunity to use mandated coverage (in one version, "single payer" nationalized health care) to improve on an unregulated equilibrium.

Distributional concerns have figured strongly in the debate as well. In addition to helping the poor, many advocate helping those with a combination of unfavorable health characteristics and poor or expensive health care insurance (the "preexisting condition problem"). Community rating is intended to serve this objective. The term *community rating* describes the regulatory requirement that an insurer who offers to sell a specified insurance contract to someone at a particular price offer the same coverage at the same price to all comers within the "community" to which that person belongs. If the community in question could be defined by the insurer, the term would connote little more than the standard practice in the industry of dividing the potentially covered population into classes within which no attempt is made to distinguish people for pricing coverage. Much more is implied when, as is intended in this context, the community is defined by the regulator.

Putting aside the geographical aspects of the definition of communities (which themselves pose interesting issues), community-rating schemes typically involve one of three kinds of discrimination:

- *No discrimination:* The community is the entire population and prices are the same for everyone.
- *Discrimination by age:* The community is the population born in a particular time period and prices may vary by date of birth.
- *Discrimination by age and gender:* The community is the male or female population born in a particular time period and prices may vary by date of birth and gender.

In this analysis, we use the term *pure community rating* to refer to the first of these schemes and a term such as *age-adjusted community rating* to refer to others. When it is clear from the context, the term *community rating*, with no modifier, means "pure community rating."

Pure community rating has been enacted into law by several states (although without the crucial requirement of mandatory purchase or provision).[1] Evidence of its appeal more broadly is the fact that it was adopted in President Clinton's Health Security Act (HSA) as the way to spread the risk of the demand for health care services across the whole society.[2] Some form of community rating (in some cases, age adjusted) was contained in almost every reform proposal introduced in the 103d Congress, a period when health care reform was at the center of attention in both Congress and the executive branch. In fact, the *Wall Street Journal* reported that "so attractive is the concept of 'community rating,' that even many Republicans and conservative Democrats say Congress should go ahead and enact it."[3] Whether health reform proceeds on an incremental basis, or a comprehensive level, as in the 103d Congress, community rating is likely to figure in the debate. Yet understanding of its implications, either for the functioning of insurance markets or for the redistributions it would imply, is scanty.

In this analysis, we focus on one of the distributional implications of a requirement of community rating. The objectives of redistributing welfare from relatively well-off to relatively poor, and from those with good health or good insurance to those with poor health and no or poor insurance, have been mentioned as possible objectives of advocates of community rating. A shift to pure community rating would, however, result in redistributions along other dimensions (for example, between people with different tastes for health care) that are, arguably, not the objectives of reformers. One such redistribution is across birth cohorts, in this case from young and future generations toward existing, especially middle-aged, birth cohorts. Given the recent concern with budget deficits and their potential effect on future generations, it is particularly important that we understand the considerable redistribution, to the disadvantage of future birth cohorts, that would occur through a switch to a system of pure community rating. Our object here is to provide quantitative estimates of this redistribution.

For purposes of our calculations, we make a critical assumption that the path of actual health care expenditures is independent of the system of financing. Some would argue that health care reform will have a large effect on this path. Advocates of a particular proposal generally claim it will produce lower outlays, while opponents may claim the reverse. We here take no position on the matter. For purposes of this exercise, we assume that between age-adjusted and pure community-rated plans there is no difference in the path of expenditures, just in the path of outlays of those who pay the bills.

Generational Consequences

The Effect of a Shift to Community Rating. The potential importance of a shift to community rating may be illustrated by some rough calculations for the case of the HSA. A study prepared for the Congressional Research Service (CRS) by the firm of Hay/Huggins estimated the average health care cost of males aged twenty-five to twenty-nine, for example, at 55 percent of the average cost of everyone in the population in 1988. The same study put the average cost of health care of a male aged sixty to sixty-four, the age of many retirees, at 200 percent of the population average in 1988.

Under pure community rating, premiums for health coverage for everyone below sixty-five would not depend on age. (Those sixty-five and older would continue to be covered by Medicare.) The common premium level would increase over time if the desired level of health care expenditures continued to rise. This complexity makes estimating the total effect difficult. But we can put a rough lower bound on the size of the transfer of burdens from older to younger and future generations if we assume there is no increase in real per capita expenditures.

In round numbers, the average premium per covered adult under the HSA was predicted to be $2,000 in 1994. (This amount would cover the adults' children. The premium in the HSA was to depend some on family status and geographical region but not on age.) The figures in the CRS report indicate that if a single premium such as this—that is, independent of age—were imposed, payments for those below their mid-forties would increase and there would be a decrease for older insureds. Combining this result with the CRS data, and with the male and female ratios in the U.S. population (as of 1991), we put the average cost of coverage in 1994 at about $1,350 for people aged twenty-five to twenty-nine; the average cost for those aged sixty to sixty-four at about $4,000. The difference between the community-rated premium and the estimated cost would result in an increase in the amount paid per year by a young person of about $650 and a decrease of $2,000 per year for a person aged sixty to sixty-four. According to these figures, the HSA would result in a roughly $26 billion increase in annual outlays by or for those between ages twenty-five and thirty-four and a $33 billion cut in annual outlays by or for those aged fifty-five to sixty-four. (For this exercise we have not tried to adjust for the relationship between family size and age, a factor that would moderate the net subsidy to the older cohorts but would not in our estimation greatly affect the conclusions.)

This calculation, however, neglects the fact that the younger group will enjoy lower premiums when they are older. No less a policy analyst than President Clinton emphasized this point: "If you have a community rating system, who gets hurt from the present system? Who pays more? Young, single, healthy people will pay more. But it's fair. You know why? Because under our system, all the young people without insurance will get insurance and because if they're young and healthy, they'll be middle aged like me some day and they'll get the benefit of this system."[4] The president is correct in pointing out that lower premiums in older years will work to offset the higher premiums the young pay early in life. It is also true that there is a level-premium system of paying for health care insurance, as in whole life insurance policies, under which the higher premium paid by a young person is actuarially fairly balanced by lower premiums he pays when older. What cannot be avoided, however, is that those generations that are older *at the time of transition* to a pure community-rated system gain and that their gain has to be made up by someone, either those who are young at the time of transition or by others yet further down the line.

Accounting for Intergenerational Transfers. The tool needed to analzye this redistribution is generational accounting, as developed by Laurence Kotlikoff and colleagues.[5] A separate chapter in the fiscal 1995 budget provides estimates of these generational burdens for 1992 and estimates the effects of the Omnibus Budget Reconciliation Act (OBRA) of 1993 and the proposed Health Security Act on these baseline estimates.[6] Table 1 displays the generational accounts, defined as the estimated present value of net payments to governments (taxes less transfers) at all levels by members of various birth cohorts over the remainder of their lives, taken from the 1995 budget.

It is important to understand the meaning of the entry in the table for "future generations." Unlike the other entries in the table, it is not a projection of any generation's actual net tax liability. Rather it is the outcome of a thought experiment, intended to give a measure of the imbalance implied by projecting existing policy. The thought experiment imposes a different system on generations born from tomorrow on, different from that actually projected for everyone currently alive. Under the different system, that uniform, net (of transfers) lifetime tax liability is imposed on all cohorts that would just barely bring into balance the intertemporal budget constraint of government, the requirement that the net present value of net payments to the government equal the sum present value of government's exhaustive expenditures and the outstanding stock of government debt. (More precisely, the thought experiment imposes a net lifetime tax liability that is the same ratio to lifetime earnings for each cohort. Earnings are typically assumed to grow at some constant rate of productivity change, so the uniform dollar amount is also thought of as growing at this rate.) This figure is comparable to the net tax burden of those aged zero in the current year, in that it refers to an entire lifetime of taxes and transfers to and from all levels of government. The larger the generational account for future generations is, in comparison with the generational account for

TABLE 1
GENERATIONAL ACCOUNTS FOR 1992 UNDER DIFFERENT POLICIES
(in thousands of dollars)

Generation's Age in 1992	Before OBRA 1993		After OBRA 1993		After the HSA	
	Male	Female	Male	Female	Male	Female
60	-48.4	-91.2	-43.9	-86.3	-35.0	-74.4
50	75.9	-2.0	81.0	2.4	91.1	15.2
40	165.2	65.0	170.9	69.1	180.3	80.1
30	196.2	93.4	201.6	96.9	209.3	103.8
20	183.0	94.2	187.7	96.9	194.7	100.1
10	121.6	65.5	124.8	67.3	130.8	68.8
0	76.4	42.9	78.4	44.1	83.2	45.8
Future generations	202.5	113.8	177.1	99.6	144.7	79.7

SOURCE: Excerpted from *Budget of the United States Government, Analytical Perspectives, Fiscal Year 1995*, Office of Management and Budget, table 3-6, p. 28.

those currently aged zero, the larger the implied passing of net tax burdens toward the future is. Although there is no scientific criterion for what the relative burdens ought to be, equality might be taken to represent a kind of distributional neutrality, implying the same average ratio of net payments to earnings for all generations, starting with those just born.

The tool of generational accounting is intended to overcome the lack of economic substance of conventional deficit accounting. Table 1 displays a typical use for this tool and shows that, according to the estimates, both OBRA 1993 and the HSA would substantially reduce the difference in net tax burdens between current and future generations by raising the total tax burden on today's living generations, especially the older generations. Focusing on the effect of the HSA, and taking the simple average of the two figures for males and females, according to table 1, the average projected net payments of those born in 1992 would have been increased by about 5 percent, or $3,250, from $61,250 by adoption of the Clinton health reform. With OBRA 1993 but without HSA, balancing the long-term budget constraint would require a net payment per person of $138,350 if living generations were held to the projected fiscal path. The HSA was projected to reduce this amount by $26,050.

The figures presented are driven by transactions that pass through the government's fiscal institutions. In the case of the HSA, the effect on the budget occurs primarily through claimed reductions in the payments for health care that result from cost containment. It is a shortcoming of conventional budgetary accounting that such calculations fail to measure the effects of policies implemented through mandates.

This point is very clearly illustrated by the case of a mandate that requires community rating of health insurance. The analysis in the budget of the generational effects of the HSA ignores the hidden, but substantial, intergenerational effects of its mandated community rating. To quantify this effect, we calculate the equivalent increment to generational accounts that the mandate would cause.

Estimating the Intergenerational Effect When People Pay Their Own Bills

A shift to a compulsory health insurance system with community rating based on age would effect some redistributions within age groups ("birth cohorts"). Healthy people and those with relatively poor health status but long-standing insurance coverage (who are therefore paying the same premiums as healthy people) would see their costs increase, while those with poorer health status or intermittent insurance coverage would see their costs decline. Pure community rating changes the payments made by (or perhaps, on behalf of—we return to this point below) people in different birth cohorts.

To estimate this effect, we start by projecting into the future the health care outlays of each already-living generation throughout its expected insured lives (which is from the present age to age sixty-five, when they become eligible for Medicare) on the assumption that each person is paying for his own health care, year by year. (An age-adjusted community rating scheme would produce the same result.) We then calculate for each generation the annual payment it would make under a pure community-rated plan, again on the assumption that each person is paying his own premiums, year by year. Expressed in per capita terms for each birth-year cohort, the discounted present value of the increase in year-by-year payments represents the effective increase in the generational account that results from a shift to community rating, all on the assumption that each person is paying his own premiums. (If the result is negative, the cohort gains from the shift.) In a second step, we repeat the analysis under the assumption that the payments on behalf of children are made by their parents.

If health care costs are on a rising path, there is what amounts to a continuing transition toward community rating. That is, there is a continuing effective shift of the burden of paying for health care toward younger and future generations. A shift to community rating decreases the amount that will be paid by those now living. As a matter of simple bookkeeping, there is a corresponding increase in the amount to be paid by everyone else, that is, those born from tomorrow on, whom we describe as "future generations." For this purpose, we treat the present as 1994, so the future generations are those born in 1995 and later. The increase in burdens on future generations is measured by the uniform payment at birth for each person born into those cohorts that would be exactly sufficient to make up the shortfall. (More precisely, the extra payment is uniform in wage units, where wages are assumed to grow at a specified uniform rate of productivity increase.) A detailed algebraic exposition of all our calculations is contained in appendix A.

Current Cost Estimates. To develop burden figures, we need a specification of the set of services to be financed and estimates of their cost. For this purpose, we have taken as a starting point the HSA proposal, which specified a benefit package and for which premium estimates were developed by the Health Care Financing Administration (HCFA). (The premium estimates are at once cost estimates, since the premium receipts were required to cover the cost of the program.)

Because the cost estimates were central to the budgetary implications of the reform proposal, and therefore politically contentious, they were subjected to a good deal of independent review. In almost every other study, the premium that would be required to cover the benefits defined in the HSA was estimated to be substantially higher than that projected by HCFA. A summary of the different estimates as reported by the Employee Benefit Research Institute is presented in table 2. As can be seen, the deviations are quite significant.

Several different methodologies were used to derive the premium estimates outlined in table 2. HCFA, Hewitt Associates, and HIAA used actuarial models combined with their own data sources to derive their estimates, while EBRI, CBO, and Wyatt used adjusted measures of national expenditures.[7] Each study made some attempt to estimate the cost of expanding coverage to the currently uninsured and the Medicaid population—a major source of the differences in each of their results.

The disparity in these estimates prompted the American Academy of Actuaries to review the methodology used by HCFA in arriving at its estimates. Among other findings, the academy work group determined that "the national average target premiums prepared by the Clinton Administration, in accordance with the constraints of the Health Security Act, may be understated by as much as 20 percent. . . . [E]stimates calculated without these constraints could range anywhere from 8 percent to 54 percent higher than the Administration's estimates."[8]

We base our projections on the assumption that costs are 15 percent higher than those implicit in the administration premium estimates for the HSA, reflecting an intermediate point in the range of differing estimates as seen in table 2. The reader can easily substitute an alternative assumption, since its effect is simply to scale up or down the estimated burdens by a simple proportion.

We used the expected alliance population as given by the American Academy of Actuaries to convert the per adult premium under the HSA to an estimated per capita premium of $1,488, considering all family types.[9] To this premium we applied the 15 percent factor discussed above, implying a per capita premium of $1,711 for 1994.

TABLE 2

SIX ESTIMATES OF 1994 PREMIUMS UNDER THE HEALTH SECURITY ACT FOR SELECTED PREMIUM CATEGORIES
(dollars)

Premium Category	HSA	CBO	EBRI	Wyatt Co.	Hewitt Assoc.	HIAA[a]
Single adult	1,932	2,100	2,202	2,285	2,440	2,610
	(100.0)	(108.7)	(114.0)	(118.3)	(126.3)	(135.0)
Couple, no children	3,865	4,200	4,404	4,570	4,880	5,219
	(100.0)	(108.7)	(113.9)	(118.2)	(126.3)	(135.0)
Single parent	3,893	4,095	4,008	4,603	4,619	4,442
	(100.0)	(105.2)	(103.0)	(118.2)	(118.6)	(114.1)
Two parent	4,360	5,565	6,210	5,155	6,946	7,153
	(100.0)	(127.6)	(142.4)	(118.2)	(159.3)	(164.1)

NOTE: In parenthesis, ratio to Health Security Act estimate in percent.
a. HIAA estimates were revised from original table to reflect an update in HIAA's estimate.
SOURCE: *Health Reform: Examining the Alternatives*, Employee Benefits Research Institute, Issue Brief 147, March 1994, table 7; *Premiums in Regional Health Alliances under the Clinton Administration Proposed Health Security Act*, Health Insurance Association of America, Actuarial memorandum, February 16, 1994 (revised). Differences calculated by the authors from the original table.

TABLE 3
ANNUAL GROWTH RATES OF HEALTH AND NONHEALTH
EXPENDITURES PER CAPITA, 1948–1998
(percent)

Period	Health	Nonhealth
1948–1958	3.9	1.6
1958–1968	5.7	2.8
1968–1978	4.6	1.5
1978–1988	4.0	1.2
1988–1998	5.5	0.3

SOURCE: Eugene Steuerle, "Health Care: But What about Everything Else," *The American Enterprise* (Jan./Feb. 1994), p. 39, table 1.

Growth in Health Care Costs over Time. Analysts have grown accustomed to thinking about the growth of health care costs in terms of the rate of growth of aggregate outlays on health care compared with the rate of growth of aggregate output, or gross domestic product (GDP). Historically, this difference has ranged from 1.2 percent in the 1950s to 3 percent in the 1980s and early 1990s. An alternative measure is the changing share of outlays on health care in the aggregate flow of goods and services, 14.3 percent of GDP in 1994. Current government baseline estimates of health expenditures expect that the ratio of health spending to GDP will stand at almost 19 percent of GDP by the year 2000, reaching over 30 percent by the year 2030.[10] If health care spending grows at a rate of 1.5 percent above the growth in GDP, health care will account for 15.4 percent of GDP in the year 2000, 22.3 percent in 2030, and almost a third of GDP by 2060. At a growth rate of 3 percent above GDP, health spending will consume 16.6 percent of GDP in 2000, reaching 55 percent of GDP by 2060.

Table 3 shows the annual growth rate of expenditures per capita on health care (and, by subtraction, on all other consumption) over various historical periods, as well as the implication of a continuation of the 3 percent gap into the further future.[11] If the trend continues, health care would constitute 76 percent of 1988–1998 growth in GDP—up from the 27 percent in the 1980s.[12]

Our approach to the range of uncertainty about the future course of health care costs is to develop projections based on alternative assumptions about the cost of providing health care to the average person of a given age. Specifically, we present estimates based on the assumptions of steady growth in this age-adjusted cost of 0, 3, and 5 percent per annum relative to the rate of growth of productivity.

A rising trend of health care's share in the value of goods and services produced (and consumed) could be the result of lagging labor productivity growth in the health care sector relative to the "all other" sector, combined with a shift in the composition of demand toward health care.[13] A shift in demand toward health care could be a consequence of rising income or of institutional factors leading to a rising standard of health care, owing to continuing development of expensive therapies.

An alternative view is that the supply of specialized resources for health care is limited, so that the market-clearing price of a given level of health care, in terms of non–health care goods and services, rises over time (this would be the sensible interpretation of the term health care cost *inflation*). These two views of the historical trends are very different, but researchers have had difficulty sorting out with confidence which is closer to the truth.[14] Our projections are agnostic on this issue. For example, 3 percent per annum would be the result of a 3 percent annual increase in the price index of a standard set of services in excess of the increase in the general wage level, with no change in the quality of services. Alternatively, it would be the result of an increase of 3 percent per annum in real services purchased, with no change in the price of health care services relative to the wage level.

Following the practice in the generational accounts presentation in the FY 1995 budget, we assume throughout that *eventually* the increase of health care costs, relative to productivity, comes to a stop. Specifically, as in the budget, we assume that after the year 2030 the rate of growth of health care cost (controlling for age) is just equal to the rate of growth of productivity.

Age Adjustments. The reason that the pure community premium for a standardized package of services differs from an age-adjusted premium is the systematic relationship between age and health care cost. To quantify this connection, we use *age adjusters*. Age adjusters, an example of the more general concept of risk adjusters,[15] express the cost of serving the population in different age classes. A profile of age adjusters that assigns, say, 4.3 to age thirty and 7.8 to age forty, would express the fact that providing the specified package of benefits to a thirty-year-old costs, on average, 4.3/7.8 = 55 percent of the cost of providing the same package to a forty-year-old.

As the example suggests, the applicable age adjusters depend on the precise specification of the associated benefit package. The HSA analysis does not provide us with such adjusters, so we have to make do with available indexes of the relative cost of serving populations of different ages. Despite the intention of several lawmakers to mandate that premiums be community rated with appropriate adjustments for age, there is little detailed public information on such adjusters. Insurance companies do use information on age in setting their premiums, but most are very reluctant to share their data because a company's ability to determine risk is a significant factor in its competitive advantage.[16] Thus, they regard their adjusters as proprietary.

We have collected adjusters from several different sources and have found overlap in the way in which different age groups are rated. The adjusters are not the same, in part, because different companies develop adjusters to reflect the specific population demographics and costs in their market areas. Another complication is that health maintenance organizations and fee-for-service insurers differ somewhat in their adjustments for different groups. HMOs, which rely on gatekeepers and practice guidelines, use much "smoother" risk adjusters, with less adjustment between groups. Finally, different insurers have different means of adjusting and accounting for different risks. One company, for example, may load the costs associated with birth into the first year after delivery, while another insurer may spread that risk over the first few years of a child's life. Figure 1 shows the age adjustment profiles from the several sets we were able to collect, using a simple average of gender-specific data.

Several government agencies have studied the relative cost and use of health care services by different age categories.[17] While such surveys are not in and of themselves considered appropriate for estimating expected cost by age, the data are broadly consistent with the different age adjusters shown in figure 1. Health care costs are high in the first few years of life because of well-baby care and other risks associated with birth. Costs stabilize around age five and remain low until age twenty. At this point, mostly because of increased risks of pregnancy in females, costs increase substantially but remain below the "average." The midpoint of risk occurs between the ages of forty and forty-nine. From this point, costs increase substantially with age, ending anywhere from four to five times the cost of health care for people in their early teens (an age when risk is at its lowest).

Table 4 gives the adjustment factors we employ in our calculations. While any one of the age adjustment estimates shown in figure 1 could have been used to provide similar results, we used an estimate that is in the public domain to allow replication of our results. These estimates are a reasonable representation of the adjusters we collected.

FIGURE 1

SAMPLE ADJUSTERS USED TO ACCOUNT FOR HEALTH
DIFFERENCES IN AGE FROM BIRTH TO AGE SIXTY-FOUR
(normalized to 1 for ages 40–44)

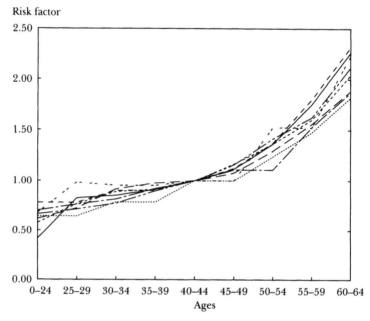

SOURCE: Proprietary information provided to authors by four insurance and consulting companies.

Demographics. As shown in figure 2, the population profile for 1995 is not evenly distributed across age cohorts
but does smooth out in later years.[18] Those aged thirty to
forty, the "baby boomers," give rise to a clear bubble in
the 1995 profile. A second bubble begins twenty years
thereafter, comprising the offspring of the baby boomers.
People born in a cohort immediately preceding a demographic bubble will benefit from having large numbers
of younger people, with relatively low health care costs,
averaged in with older generations to lower the community-rated premium. Those born immediately after the

TABLE 4

THE RELATIONSHIP OF HEALTH STATUS TO AGE AS EXPRESSED
BY ADJUSTMENT FACTOR, BIRTH THROUGH AGE SIXTY-FOUR

Age	Factor	Age	Factor
0–24	0.63	45–49	1.10
25–29	0.68	50–54	1.35
30–34	0.73	55–59	1.55
35–39	0.85	60–64	2.00
40–44	0.95	65 +	Medicare

SOURCE: Calculated from a report by the Congressional Research Service and Hay Huggins, Inc., 1988.

bubble suffer from having larger cohorts of older people included in their average when their community-rated premium is calculated. This effect is somewhat offset by the trailing bubble.

The population data we employed originated with the Social Security Administration, whose projections extend into the middle of the next century.[19] Jagadeesh Gokhale, who provided us with an extensive data set tracking population by age and sex through 2200, extrapolated projections past the Social Security Administration's estimates by continuing the various population trends present at the tail end of the administration's data. We used the Gokhale data through 2080 to estimate burdens on identified birth cohorts. To compute the burden on future generations, we require an assumed rate of population growth for the years beyond 2080. For this purpose, we use the average growth rate of the newborn population in the Gokhale data for the years 2071–2080 (0.733 percent).

To calculate the change in net payment into the system by those who are born after 1994 ("future generations"), we determined the constant amount (in terms of earning power; the payment in the exercise grows at the rate of productivity increase) that, if paid at birth by each

FIGURE 2
POPULATION PROFILE BY AGE AND SEX, 1995–2055

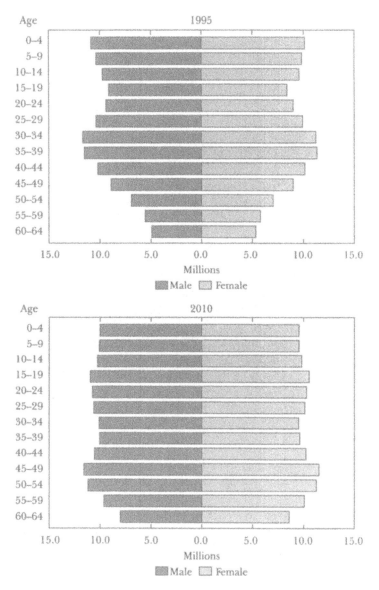

FIGURE 2 (continued)

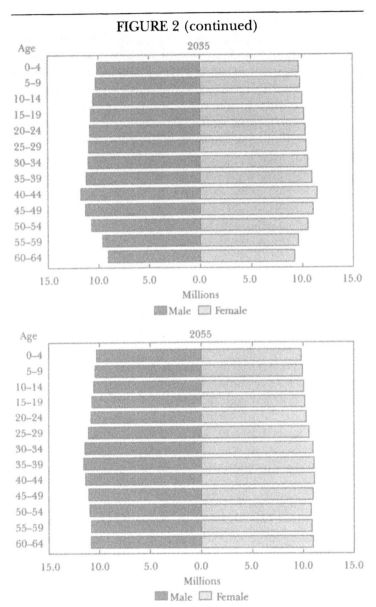

SOURCE: Social Security Administration projections provided to the authors by Jagadeesh Gokhale.

newborn, would exactly cover the difference between the stream of payments he will make under the community-rated system and what he would have had to pay under the status quo ante system. This calculation is a measure of the amount that will be *saved* by living generations, in total, by the shift in policy. In an ongoing system, the excess is forever passed along to those born in the yet further future. Our calculation is designed to determine the effect of stopping the passing of the buck and sharing the problem equally over all generations born from tomorrow forward.

It should be emphasized that this net payment is a *hypothetical* quantity, designed to provide a concrete measure of the extent to which the shift in systems transfers a burden toward the future. It is the exact analogue of the generational account of "future generations" in table 1 and should be compared both with that figure and with the amounts for those who are aged zero, that is, born in 1994, in our tables. As in the case of generational accounts, a possible standard of distributional neutrality between current newborns and future generations would be equality of this lifetime excess of payments over health care received. But our attention focuses equally on the redistribution from younger living generations toward older living generations, especially the middle-aged. (In our central case, all cohorts aged thirty and older in 1994 gain from the shift, and the largest gain goes to those aged fifty.)

A word about immigration: the population projections on which we have relied incorporate immigration. In projecting the cost of the system and the payments by the various living cohorts, immigrants have been included. By contrast, in calculating the hypothetical net effect on future generations of making the change from pay-your-own-way to community rating, we have placed the burden of balancing the system on the sequence of newborns, starting in 1995. It is difficult to say whether the result is biased up or down. If immigrants arrive as young people, they help out by chipping in more than they cost. If they arrive as older people, they add to the problem. We did not consider the possible gain from attempting to deal systematically with this problem worth the cost.

Discount Rate. Present-value calculations rely heavily on the estimation of an appropriate discount rate. The generational accounts presented in the budget are based on a real discount rate of 6 percent, roughly the midpoint between the real historical rate on federal government bonds and the average real return to private sector capital (which includes a premium for risk). We present results for real discount rates of 3, 6, and 9 percent.

Results. Figure 3 shows the difference in net payments in year 1 (assuming start-up in 1994) between the pure community-rated system and an age-adjusted community-rated premium, by age of the insured. This figure conveys the effect of the imposition of community rating on the initial year's cash flow, a substantial decrease in payments by older cohorts, made up by increases in payments by younger cohorts.[20] The increased payments by younger cohorts are, to a degree, compensated when they themselves are older. The decreased payments by older cohorts upon introduction of pure community rating constitute a pure windfall gain to them and are not compensated for by subsequently larger payments.

Figure 4 shows the expected path of payments for people born in 1945, 1965, 1995, and 2015 as it would unfold were the system to continue unchanged until those cohorts have reached the age of Medicare eligibility under the assumption of zero growth in health care costs and zero productivity growth. Also shown is the path of the expected community-rated premium. Because health care costs are assumed constant, the variation in the

FIGURE 3

Net Difference between Pure Community-rated Premium and Age-adjusted Premium in 1994, Total in Age Cohort, Birth to Age Sixty-four
(millions of dollars)

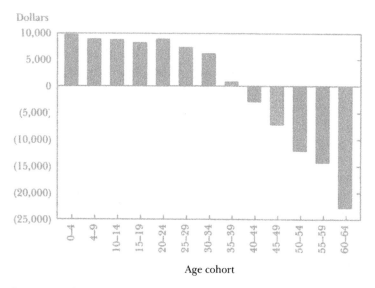

Age cohort

Source: Authors' calculations.

community-rated premium results only from changes in the demographic profile of the population over time. This figure makes clear that people born in 1945 are certain winners (always assuming no change in the quality of coverage) in that the required payment under community rating is always below the age-adjusted payment that would be required in the status quo. Likewise, the figure shows the expected path of gains and losses in cash-flow terms for those born in 1965, 1995, and 2015. The longer the path remains above the community-rated premium, the greater the benefits are from a shift away from age-adjusted rating.

FIGURE 4

LIFETIME AGE-ADJUSTED PREMIUM PAYMENTS AND THE ESTIMATED COMMUNITY-RATED PREMIUM OVER TIME, 1995–2075

(in 1994 labor units)

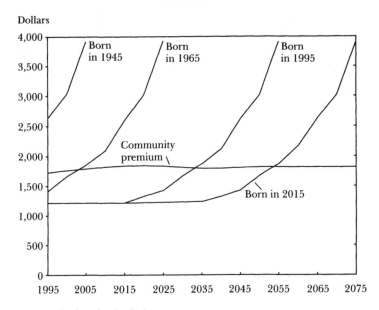

SOURCE: Authors' calculations.

Table 5 summarizes the effect on various generations of a shift to community rating as of January 1, 1994, under the assumption of a 0.75 percent annual growth in productivity and a range of assumptions about the applicable real discount rate and the path of health care costs. The calculations treat insurance payments as made in full at the beginning of each year. The entries for the various ages can be thought of as additions to the generational accounts, defined as the present value of net payments (so a negative sign represents an improvement in position), as of 1994. An exception is the entry for the generation born in 2015, which represents the addition to the life-

TABLE 5
PRESENT VALUE OF NET PER CAPITA PAYMENTS UNDER SHIFT TO
COMMUNITY RATING
(thousands of 1994 dollars)

Generation's Age in 1994	Growth of Relative Cost of Health Care		
	0.00	0.03	0.05
60	−9.7	−10.3	−10.7
50	−13.8	−17.3	−20.2
40	−9.8	−15.4	−21.0
30	−3.8	−10.0	−17.8
20	1.9	−2.8	−10.5
10	5.8	4.8	1.7
0	8.2	10.8	12.6
Future generations	9.0	19.4	33.4
Born in 2015	9.4	22.6	40.5

NOTE: Assuming 0.75 percent productivity growth and 6 percent real discount.
SOURCE: Authors' calculations.

time net tax liability of that generation measured as of its date of birth (treating the increment to health care costs due to the shift to community rating as a tax), deflated for the productivity growth from 1994 to 2015 to make it comparable to the figure for the age zero cohort in 1994. It is a *projection* made under the assumption that the community-rated system remains in place through their lifetimes.

For what we take as central case assumptions (discount rate of 6 percent, health care cost growth rate, through 2030, of 3 percent, relative to productivity growth of 0.75 percent), the shift to community rating is estimated to generate a gain of $17,300 per person aged fifty in 1994. The gainers extend to those somewhere between ages ten and twenty, where the break-even age is found. Those born in 1994 are handed an extra payment obligation with a discounted value of $10,800 each. These figures may be compared with generational accounts as of

1992 (averaged over males and females) of ($81,000 + $2,400)/2 = $41,700 for the fifty-year-olds, and ($78,400 + $44,100)/2 = $61,250 for the newborns, in the base case (after OBRA 1993) presented in table 1.

By contrast, the figures shown in table 5 for future generations refer not to a projection but rather to the hypothetical burden measure discussed above. The central case estimate of $19,400 may be compared with the generational account estimate for future generations as of 1992 (for the same baseline policy) of ($177,100 + $99,600)/2 = $138,350. The figures make clear that the regulatory policy shift, with no direct budgetary implications, is large in its intergenerational transfer effect in comparison with many policy options considered within the usual budgetary framework.

For the case with low growth of relative health care costs, while some recapture of benefits occurs for younger people and for those to be born in the future, those persons will not completely recapture the windfall gained by older generations. An increase in the rate of growth of health care costs has two effects. First, an increase in the scale of the entire stream of payments tends to raise both the pre- and the postpolicy change figures for all cohorts. Second, because community rating forces younger generations to share the costs at the point when those costs are relatively high, the shift to community rating works to the advantage of everyone living at the time of transition, relative to future generations, the higher the growth rate of health care costs. In effect, a new shift to community rating happens every year, so that the higher costs of health care in old age are moved forward to future younger generations.

The effect of that shift can be seen in table 6, which is based on a zero rate of discount. In this case, *all* living generations gain, even the 2015 generation, by virtue of spreading the cost of health care over growing numbers of people in the further future, regardless of the rate of

TABLE 6
PRESENT VALUE OF NET PER CAPITA PAYMENTS UNDER SHIFT TO COMMUNITY RATING
(thousands of 1994 dollars)

Generation's Age in 1994	Growth of Relative Cost of Health Care		
	0.00	0.03	0.05
60	−10.7	−11.4	−11.9
50	−20.6	−26.4	−31.4
40	−21.9	−36.5	−51.6
30	−19.1	−45.8	−80.5
20	−15.0	−53.4	−111.9
10	−8.8	−45.4	−104.9
0	−2.4	−30.3	−78.3
Born in 2015	−0.9	−8.2	−22.1

NOTE: Assuming 0 percent productivity growth and 0 percent real discount.
SOURCE: Authors' calculations.

growth of health care costs, with very large gains evident for the young and the 2015 cohort at a growth rate of health care costs of 5 percent. Because it appears in this case that the change in the system creates only winners (whereas, in fact, a large and growing burden is being passed to the further future), table 6 demonstrates the importance of bringing into the picture the "future generations" calculation in table 5. (We do not show a figure for future generations in this table because the required series for the calculation does not converge with a zero rate of discount.)

Accounting for Third-Party Payers in the Status Quo and Community-rated Systems

The Effect of Third-Party Payers. The calculations above incorporate the assumption that in the status quo ante everyone pays his own health care bills, year by year, and everyone pays his own community-rated premium each year in the community-rated system. In actuality, for many people, health care bills are paid by third parties in the status quo ante, as would probably be true in a community-rated system as well.

To assess the implications of this possibility for the intergenerational distributive effects of a shift in systems, we consider various prominent categories of third parties.

Insurance companies. People buying health insurance privately, year by year, to cover their own health care costs are, in effect, paying their own bills in their current premiums. For these people, the shift to community rating would seem to be reasonably described by the analysis above.

If people were to obtain health care coverage on the basis of fixed price—the analogue would be level-premium life insurance—a shift to community rating would affect the insuring entity, for example, the owners of an insurance company. This situation does not appear to be common. A variant does, however, prevail for retirees receiving guaranteed benefits from their companies. Variation in the cost of serving such people falls on the owners of the guaranteeing companies. A shift to a community-rated system would benefit these owners if it enabled them to purchase coverage for their beneficiaries in the private market at the community premium.

Our focus in this volume is national community rating, with obligatory purchase of insurance, implemented through regulation. As has been mentioned, several states have imposed community rating at various times in the past.[21] One might think that adding a federal requirement would cause no fresh intergenerational distributions in these jurisdictions. The state regulations, however, do *not* impose obligatory purchase of insurance. Theory suggests that such a rule will induce people against whom such a pricing scheme works, such as young people and healthy people, to leave the pool. As a consequence, the intergenerational distribution that would have resulted from the state rules would have been reduced. A federal rule with mandatory purchase would then compel the participation of the young and would result in intergenerational redistribution along the lines developed above, although perhaps moderated to some degree.

Employers. For people obtaining health care insurance from their employers as a part of their compensation packages, the story is more complicated. Employees may pay nothing for their insurance, or they may pay an amount that is independent of age (although it may depend on family status). Because the insurance coverage is implicitly priced in the terms of employment, it is very difficult to determine who "really" pays. The question is whether the age profile implicit in the compensation of employees mimics the age profile of health care premiums characteristic of the competitive insurance market.

Under competitive pressure, most commercial insurance is experience or demographically rated. Table 7 presents estimates prepared by the American Academy of Actuaries of the rating method currently used in the privately insured market. As the table shows, only 15 million or 10 percent of the total privately insured population of 157 million falls under a purely (unadjusted) community rate, with the remainder covered under methods that may be presumed to have the effect of age adjustment. These data, however, concern the cost of insurance to the employer. Even under experience rating, community rating may exist within firms purchasing insurance for their employees. While insurance sold to a large company may be priced on the experience of that company, for example, it is likely to be provided to the individual employees on a community-rated basis—using the company as the community. This arrangement is often known as intracompany community rating. The extent to which intracompany community rating translates into effective

TABLE 7

ESTIMATED NONELDERLY POPULATION BY HEALTH INSURANCE, 1993
(in millions)

Market Segment	Current Rating Method			Total Insured Lives
	Pure community rating	Community rating by class	Other rating method	
Employer Sponsored				
Fewer than 25 employees	5	10	6	21
25–99 employees	3	8	7	18
100–999 employees	2	11	18	31
More than 1,000 employees	2	5	62	69
Total employees sponsored	12	34	93	139
Individual insurance	3	6	9	18
Total private insured	15	40	102	157

SOURCE: *An Analysis of Mandated Community Rating*, American Academy of Actuaries, September 2, 1993 (revision to March 22, 1993 report), p. 3.

community rating for the work force depends on whether the terms of employment adjust to reflect the different value of health insurance to workers with different characteristics. Such an adjustment could result from a sorting of workers into different companies according to health status and from a tendency for compensation to vary with age in the population. Sherry Glied has argued that recent market changes have caused firms and individuals to base employment decisions on the health status of the individual or on the insurance a given firm may offer.[22] A sorting of workers into firms based on risk has therefore occurred. Furthermore, as more firms begin to offer multiple health insurance plans for their employees, risk is further homogenized. A recent contribution by Louise Sheiner[23] summarizes the literature and presents new evidence of the validity of the economists' presumption that employees "pay for" employer-provided health insurance.

Governments. Apart from their role as employers, governments provide health care to various groups. Most obviously, the federal Medicare program provides hospital care and subsidized physician care to people aged sixty-five and older. In addition, government finances health care for people with particular health conditions (for example, black lung disease or kidney failure) and in particular economic circumstances. The federal-state Medicaid program, for example, covers low-income people. Relative to the population aged zero to sixty-four, the beneficiaries of Medicaid are concentrated among children and young mothers, and those paying the bills are a cross-section of taxpayers. Providing for a compulsory national community-rated insurance system would presumably result in a shift of the burden of financing the system from somewhat older taxpayers to somewhat younger payers of the community-rated premium.

Parents. In the context of our analysis earlier in this volume, parents are "third-party payers" on behalf of their children. It is possible that the ultimate burden of variation in health care costs paid for by parents is shifted by offsetting variation in other transfers from parents to children. Generational accounting is, by convention, silent on the question of the ultimate incidence of payments by generations. Generational accounts record estimates of the discounted values of net payments by different cohorts (normally, to governments, in this case to health care providers or insurance companies). As in the case of variation in payments by a cohort to governments (for example, resulting from a tax cut or tax increase), variation in payments to the health care system may result in offsetting adjustments to intergenerational transfers. In this sense, generational accounts, and our analysis, record "impact effects" of policy changes.

Adjusting the Calculations to a "Parents-Pay" Basis. To account for the fact that parents pay the bills for their children, we reallocate the payments, both before and after the policy change, for cohorts aged zero to eighteen, to older cohorts. Thus, we confine the payers of health care costs to those aged nineteen and up. For this purpose, we take the distribution of ages of mothers in 1990 as the distribution of ages of mothers of newborns in all years. (Strictly speaking, the distribution of ages of mothers in a given year includes the influence of the demographic history, which affects the distribution and fertility of women of different ages in the population.) Since the object is to allocate payments to responsible adults, rather than to mothers, and since fathers are, on average, about two years older than mothers, to approximate the distribution of the average age of parents, we used our derived distribution of mothers' ages, shifted by one year. Eliminating the tails of the distribution, with very small weight, gave us a span of ages of parents from sixteen to forty-five at the time of the birth of the child. To determine the pattern of payments under the "parents-pay" version of the analysis, we reallocate the payments determined under the "own pay" version, described earlier, to the respective older cohorts. This calculation requires two rounds of reallocation. In the first round, the payments by cohorts aged zero to fifteen are allocated to those sixteen to forty-five years older. This number adds to the payments made by those aged sixteen and older. In the second round, the payments of those aged sixteen, seventeen, and eighteen are allocated to those sixteen to forty-five years older than they are. The resulting payment profile is thus 0 for those aged zero to eighteen and is higher than the "own pay" amount for those aged nineteen to sixty-three. In effect, the bills of the youngest parents, those aged sixteen to eighteen, are further reallocated to their parents, who are the grandparents of the youngest of the children in the analysis.

Results. Table 8, corresponding to table 5 for the pay-your-own-way assumptions, summarizes for the parents-pay assumptions the effect on various generations of a shift to community rating as of January 1, 1994, under the central case assumption of a 0.75 percent annual growth in productivity and a range of assumptions about the applicable real discount rate and the path of health care costs. (Appendix B provides a tabular presentation of a wide range of alternative assumptions about key parameters.)

It will be seen that, as would be expected, the parents-pay assumptions result in smaller intergenerational transfer effects from the shift to community rating. For the central case (discount rate of 6 percent, growth rate of health care costs through 2030 of 3 percent, relative to productivity growth of 0.75 percent), the shift to community rating is estimated to generate a gain of $16,700 (versus $17,300 under pay-your-own way assumptions) per person aged fifty in 1994. The break-even age is increased from somewhere between ages ten and twenty

TABLE 8
PRESENT VALUE OF NET PER CAPITA PAYMENTS UNDER SHIFT TO
COMMUNITY RATING WHEN PARENTS PAY FOR CHILDREN
(thousands of 1994 dollars)

Generation's Age in 1994	Growth of Relative Cost of Health Care		
	0.00	0.03	0.05
60	−9.7	−10.3	−10.7
50	−13.3	−16.7	−19.5
40	−7.2	−12.5	−17.8
30	1.0	−3.8	−10.5
20	7.7	6.3	2.0
10	5.5	7.6	8.5
0	3.4	7.1	11.6
Future generations	3.5	9.4	18.0
Born in 2015	3.5	10.0	19.9

NOTE: Assuming 0.75 percent productivity growth and 6 percent real discount.
SOURCE: Authors' calculations.

to somewhere between ages twenty and thirty. Those born in 1994 are handed an extra payment obligation with a discounted value of $7,100 (versus $10,800) each. The central case "future generations" estimate is substantially reduced, from $19,400 to $9,400.

Conclusion

It is a poorly appreciated fact that mandates and other regulations, which are not accounted for in the government's budget, can duplicate the effect of spending and tax-transfer programs, which are. Important examples are to be found in the recent health care reform debate in the United States. Interestingly, official agencies recognized that mandating the provision by employers of insurance to their employees was equivalent to a tax on employers to pay for a transfer to employees. It was, however, little noticed that the contemplated mandate that insurance companies provide health insurance on a community-rated basis would amount to an implicit addition to the federal deficit in effecting transfers of income toward older generations, at the expense of younger and future birth cohorts.

Using data from a variety of sources, we conclude that the effect would be substantial. The magnitudes depend on assumptions about discount, health care cost, and productivity growth rates. The effect also depends on who is responsible for paying the health care bills of children. Under the assumption that parents pay for their children (which moderates the intergenerational transfer) and our central case assumptions about the discount, cost, and productivity growth rates, we estimate that a shift to community rating would generate gains for people over age thirty in 1994, $16,700 per person aged fifty for example, at the cost to younger cohorts. Those born in 1994 would acquire an extra payment obligation with a discounted value of $7,100 each. The burden passed along to future generations can be described as a $9,300 per capita tax at birth (growing with productivity).

The analysis makes clear that the regulatory policy shift, with no direct budgetary implications, would have an intergenerational transfer effect comparable to what would be considered a major change in on-budget tax or transfer programs.

Algebraic Description of the Calculations

Let the variable $P_{t,k}$ stand for the population in year t of people born in year k, $N_{t,k}$ the net payment they make for health insurance in year t, and $G_{t,k}$ the cost of providing covered health care to them. $N_{t,k}$ depends on the system of pricing insurance, for example, the choice between community-rated and unregulated private market systems, and on the identity of the payers under whatever pricing scheme exists. $G_{t,k}$ is taken as the same for all alternative insurance regimes, but we consider alternative paths. The analysis in the book consists of working out the implications of the choice of payment regime for the discounted value of payments by each generation.

The key parameters are the real rate of discount, r, the rate of productivity growth, g, and the rate of growth, h, in health care outlay per person. The latter is, in turn, specified by its rate of growth, h_r, relative to earnings, so $h = h_r + g$. These parameters are assigned alternative values to specify scenarios. The parameters r and g are treated as constants for each scenario. We consider 3 percent, 6 percent, and 9 percent for r, 0 percent, and 0.25 percent, 0.75 percent, and 1.25 percent for g. Following the treatment of health care expenditures for purposes of the generational accounting presented in the FY 1995 budget, we limit the period of relative increase in health care outlays per person to the period up until the year 2030. So h_r

is assigned alternative values 0 percent, 3 percent, and 5 percent until 2030 and 0 after that. Our central case is r = 6 percent, h_l = 3 percent (until 2030), and g = 0.75 percent.

An additional parameter, n, the rate of growth of the cohorts of newborns beyond the last year for which we have explicit projections (the year 2080), is derived by projection from the last ten years of the data and has value n = 0.733 percent. (The numbers of people of each age from 2080 on is determined by assuming that the ratio to the number of newborns is the same as in 2080, so numbers of people of each age are assumed to grown at n after 2080.)

Determining the Population at Each Time. The populations, $P_{t,k}$, for t = 1994, . . . 2080 and k < 2081, are data. For t > 2080 and all $k \leq t$, we assume

$$P_{t,k} = P_{2080,2080 + k - t}(1 + n)^{t - 2080}.$$

Determining the Cost of Serving a Generation in a Particular Year. We assume that the cost of serving a person depends only on the person's age, a, and the year. The dependence on age is expressed through the concept of an age adjuster, w_a. As described in the body of the book, the scale value of w_a is arbitrary: w_{26}/w_{40} describes the cost of serving a twenty-six-year-old relative to the cost of serving a forty-year-old. Given a profile of age adjusters, we can identify the "standard cost," SC, of health care as the cost of serving a person with an age adjuster equal to 1. Readers may find it helpful to think of age adjusters as ranged around the value of 1 for the person with middling health care cost. Among people below age sixty-five, that middling level would be somewhere between ages forty and forty-five. If the age adjuster profile assigns value 1 at age forty-five, the other weights, determined empirically, would, in fact, range from approximately .6 for ages zero to twenty-four to 2 for ages sixty to sixty-four. With this choice of units, the standard cost is the cost of serving a forty-five-year-old. The weights we actually used, given in table 4, have roughly this interpretation. But it should be emphasized that the choice of the scale of weights is arbitrary and that the standardized cost is specified relative to the particular choice of scale.

Once a profile of age adjusters has been determined, we can define the total age-adjusted equivalent population, $TAAE_t$, as the age-adjuster weighted average of the actual population at time t:

$$TAAE_t = \sum_k w_{t-k} P_{t,k}.$$

$TAAE_t$ can be thought of as the number of forty-five-year-olds that are equivalent, from a health care cost point of view, to the actual population at time t.

The standardized cost of covered health care for 1994 is determined from data. Specifically, as discussed in the text, we took as a datum the community-rated premium in the HSA, increased by 15 percent to allow for underestimation by HCFA, multiplied by the population in 1994. Dividing this by $TAAE_{1994}$ gives us SC_{1994}. Subsequently,

$$SC_t = SC_{1994}(1 + h_l + g)^{t-1994},$$

where recall that h_l is a specified constant through 2030 and 0 after that.

The cost of serving in year t the generation born in year k is then given by

$$G_{t,k} = w_{t-k} SC_t P_{t,k}.$$

Determining the Health Insurance Premiums. In the text, we distinguish two methods of determining premiums, unregulated or, equivalently for our purposes, age-adjusted community rating (here designated by the superscript *ACR*) and pure community rating (*PCR*). The age-adjusted community-rated premium at time t for a person born in year k is thus

$$P_{t,k}^{ACR} = w_{t-k}SC_t.$$

The pure community-rated premium for a person in year t is found by dividing the total cost of serving the population in a given year by the size of the population:

$$P_t^{PCR} = \sum_k G_{t,k} \bigg/ \sum_k \mathrm{P}_{t,k}.$$

Determining the Payment by a Generation in a Given Year. In the text we distinguish two payment regimes according to who pays the bills of children—pay their own (*OP*) or parents pay (*PP*). So, for example, the amount paid in year t by members of the generation born in k with pure community rating when each cohort is regarded as responsible for its own bills would be designated $N_{t,k}^{PCR,OP}$.

The pay-your-own-way case. Our focus is on the difference between age-adjusted community rating and pure community rating under each of the two possibilities for the responsibility for payment. The net increase in payment for health care incurred in year t by people aged a as a result of shifting from *ACR* to *PCR* when everyone is regarded as paying his own bills is, for example, $p_t^{PCR} - p_{t,t-a}^{ACR}$. A typical point in figure 3 would be $p_{1994}^{PCR} - p_{1994,1950}^{ACR}$, allowing 1950 to stand for the birth year of those aged forty to forty-four in the grouped data.

The aggregate increase in payments in year t by people aged a as a result of shifting from *ACR* to *PCR* when everyone is regarded as paying his own bills is given by

$$N_{t,t-a}^{PCR,OP} - N_{t,t-a}^{ACR,OP} = P_{t,t-a}(p_t^{PCR} - p_{t,t-a}^{ACR}).$$

This is the amount that is discounted to 1994 and divided by the population of the various ages in the typical entry of table 5. Define as the per capita "net assessment," A, in year t on the generation born in year k then living, resulting from a shift in regime, for example, from *ACR* to *PCR*, the discounted (to t) value of the increase in net annual payments over their lifetimes. Notice that to identify a net assessment we need to specify the regime shift (so two items of information), the identity of the payers, the year, and the generation. For most of our exposition, the regime shift and identity of the payers will be clear from the context. But the following example, for the generation aged forty in 1994, will illustrate the concept and the calculations:

$$A^{PCR,ACR,OP}_{1994,1954} = \frac{\displaystyle\sum_{t=1994}^{1994+64-40} (1+r)^{1994-t}\left(N^{PCR,OP}_{t,1994-40} - N^{ACR,OP}_{t,1994-40} \right)}{P_{1994,1954}},$$

where the sum is taken out to the point where those aged forty in 1994 reach Medicare eligibility at age sixty-five.

The calculation for the generation born in 2015 is taken back to its year of birth. For comparability with those born in 1994, the result is then deflated by the productivity growth between 1994 and 2015, so that the quantity can be understood in terms of the same earning power. So the expression in the table is

$(1+g)^{1994-2015} A_{2015,2015}$

$$= (1+g)^{1994-2015}\left[\frac{\displaystyle\sum_{t=2015}^{2015+64} (1+r)^{2015-t}\left(N^{PCR,OP}_{t,2015} - N^{ACR,OP}_{t,2015} \right)}{P_{2015,2015}} \right].$$

The parents-pay case. In assigning the payments due from children to their parents, we first determine statistically what age a parent of a newborn is likely to be, given a total natality sample that has been truncated to fit mothers' ages fifteen through forty-four.[24] Assuming that fathers are, on average, two years older than mothers, we use these ages to approximate ages of parents sixteen to forty-five. The data then give us the number of parents, a_i of each age, i, sixteen through forty-five, from which we derive the vector of resulting constants, b_{16} to b_{45}, summing to 1, that can be thought of as the distribution of ages of the people responsible for the bills of a randomly chosen newborn until age eighteen:

$$
\begin{bmatrix} a_{16} \\ a_{17} \\ a_{18} \\ ... \\ a_{45} \end{bmatrix} = \left(\sum_{i=16}^{45} a_i \right) \times \begin{bmatrix} b_{16} \\ b_{17} \\ b_{18} \\ ... \\ b_{45} \end{bmatrix}.
$$

The extra payment in year t made on behalf of children, $EB_{t,k}$ by a member of the generation born in year k, is the weighted sum of payments made under the pay-your-own-way assumption for the younger generations. The formula for the pure community-rating case, for example, is:

$$
EB_{t,k}^{PCR} = \sum_{i=16}^{45} b_i N_{t,k-i}^{PCR,OP}.
$$

Two passes through the data are made, reassigning first the payments of ages fifteen and under to their parents and second the total burdens borne by the parents who are aged sixteen to eighteen. The end result is that children of ages zero to eighteen are not held accountable for gains or losses, while parents of up to age sixty-three have seen their payments grow as a result of the shifting.

The Hypothetical Future Generations' Payment. The calculation for the "future generations' " net payment has a similar structure. The discounted excess of amounts paid by living generations under the age-adjusted community rating over what they pay under pure community rating must, as a matter of intertemporal budget constraint, be covered, in present value, by payments of generations not yet living. It is a straightforward matter to calculate this excess, which we label the "passed burden," *PB*. But rather than make a prediction about how the long-term budget constraint will be satisfied, the hypothetical thought experiment is to determine "future generations' assessment" at *t*, FA_t, a flat (in terms of earnings) assessment on each newborn, starting in year $t+1$, that would be paid just sufficient to balance the books. Adorned with superscripts to specify precisely the policy shift and payment assumption involved, it is thus defined implicitly by:

$$\sum_{t'=t+1}^{\infty} FA_t^{PCR,ACR,OP} (1+g)^{t'-t}(1+r)^{t-t'} P_{t',t'} = PB_t^{PCR,ACR,OP},$$

which can be solved as

$$FA_t^{PCR,ACR,OP} = \frac{PB_t^{PCR,ACR,OP}}{\sum_{t'=t+1}^{\infty} (1+g)^{t'-t}(1+r)^{t-t'} P_{t',t'}}.$$

The numerator in this expression is the change in burden passed forward as a result of the specified regime shift. The demoninator is a kind of discounted stream of newborns. In computing the denominator, we need to use the long-run growth rate of the population. For the typical entry in our tables, the calculation is given by

$$FA_{1994} =$$

$$\frac{PB_{1994}}{\sum_{t=1994}^{2079} \dfrac{P_{t+1,t+1}(1+g)^{t-1994}}{(1+r)^{t-1994}} + \sum_{t=2080}^{\infty} \dfrac{P_{2080,2080}(1+n)^{t-2080}(1+g)^{t-1994}}{(1+r)^{t-1994}}},$$

where the superscripts have been suppressed. Provided that $(1+n)(1+g) < (1+r)$, the requirement for convergence of the infinite series in the demoninator, FA_{1994}, will be defined.

APPENDIX B:
A SENSITIVITY ANALYSIS OF THE PRESENT VALUE OF NET PAYMENTS UNDER A SHIFT TO COMMUNITY RATING

Parameters (percent)			Born in 2015	Future genera-tions	Cohort Pays Own Bills						
g	h_t	r			0	10	20	30	40	50	60
0.25	0	3	9.7	9.2	8.4	3.8	-2.0	-8.4	-14.1	-16.6	-10.2
		6	9.1	8.8	7.9	5.9	2.3	-3.2	-9.1	-13.4	-9.7
		9	7.3	6.9	6.3	5.4	3.3	-0.9	-6.1	-11.0	-9.2
	3	3	23.1	21.7	7.5	-3.8	-14.9	-20.6	-22.8	-21.0	-10.8
		6	21.9	18.6	10.6	5.5	-1.5	-8.6	-14.2	-16.7	-10.2
		9	17.2	13.2	8.5	6.3	2.3	-3.3	-9.3	-13.5	-9.7
	5	3	41.0	39.1	3.0	-17.8	-34.9	-36.3	-31.7	-24.7	-11.2
		6	39.4	31.7	12.8	3.3	-7.8	-15.5	-19.4	-19.4	-10.6
		9	30.4	21.1	10.6	6.7	0.5	-6.5	-12.4	-15.6	-10.0

Parents Pay

Parameters (percent)			Born in 2015	Future genera-tions	0	10	20	30	40	50	60
g	h_t	r									
0.25	0	3	4.8	4.7	4.5	5.8	6.4	−2.5	−11.2	−16.0	−10.2
		6	3.2	3.2	3.1	5.2	7.7	1.4	−6.6	−12.8	−9.6
		9	1.7	1.7	1.7	3.7	7.1	2.9	−3.9	−10.5	−9.2
	3	3	13.7	12.9	8.3	4.5	−1.3	−12.9	−19.5	−20.3	−10.8
		6	9.1	8.5	6.6	7.5	6.9	−2.7	−11.4	−16.1	−10.2
		9	4.8	4.4	3.6	5.7	7.9	1.3	−6.8	−13.0	−9.7
	5	3	27.4	25.0	11.9	−1.2	−15.8	−26.9	−28.0	−24.0	−11.2
		6	18.2	16.4	10.8	8.9	3.7	−8.5	−16.3	−18.8	−10.6
		9	9.7	8.3	5.9	7.6	7.9	−1.0	−9.7	−15.0	−10.0

(Table continues)

APPENDIX B: (Continued)

Cohort Pays Own Bills

Parameters (percent)			Born in 2015	Future generations	0	10	20	30	40	50	60
g	h_i	r									
0.75	0	3	9.2	8.5	7.8	2.8	-3.4	-9.8	-15.2	-17.2	-10.3
		6	9.4	9.0	8.2	5.8	1.9	-3.8	-9.8	-13.8	-9.7
		9	7.6	7.2	6.6	5.5	3.2	-1.2	-6.5	-11.4	-9.3
	3	3	21.4	20.1	5.0	-7.6	-19.1	-23.7	-24.8	-21.8	-10.9
		6	22.6	19.4	10.8	4.8	-2.8	-10.0	-15.4	-17.3	-10.3
		9	17.9	13.9	8.9	6.4	2.0	-4.0	-10.0	-14.0	-9.8
	5	3	37.4	36.4	-2.8	-25.8	-43.2	-41.7	-34.5	-25.7	-11.3
		6	40.5	33.4	12.6	1.7	-10.5	-17.8	-21.0	-20.2	-10.7
		9	31.7	22.4	11.1	6.5	-0.4	-7.5	-13.4	-16.1	-10.1

Parents Pay

Parameters (percent)			Born in 2015	Future generations	0	10	20	30	40	50	60
g	h_t	r									
0.75	0	3	4.7	4.5	4.5	5.5	5.6	−3.7	−12.3	−16.6	−10.3
		6	3.5	3.5	3.4	5.5	7.7	1.0	−7.2	−13.3	−9.7
		9	1.9	1.9	1.9	3.9	7.2	2.7	−4.3	−10.9	−9.3
	3	3	13.6	12.3	7.5	2.4	−4.3	−15.7	−21.4	−21.2	−10.9
		6	10.0	9.4	7.1	7.6	6.3	−3.8	−12.5	−16.7	−10.3
		9	5.4	4.9	4.0	6.1	8.0	0.8	−7.4	−13.4	−9.8
	5	3	27.0	24.0	9.6	−6.3	−22.3	−31.9	−30.7	−25.0	−11.3
		6	19.9	18.0	11.6	8.5	2.0	−10.5	−17.8	−19.5	−10.7
		9	10.8	9.3	6.6	8.0	7.6	−1.9	−10.6	−15.6	−10.1

(Table continues)

APPENDIX B: (Continued)

Cohort Pays Own Bills

Parameters (percent)			Born in 2015	Future generations	0	10	20	30	40	50	60
g	h_t	r									
1.25	0	3	8.3	7.0	6.8	1.3	−5.2	−11.4	−16.5	−17.9	−10.4
		6	9.7	9.3	8.4	5.7	1.4	−4.5	−10.5	−14.4	−9.8
		9	7.9	7.5	6.9	5.6	3.1	−1.5	−7.0	−11.8	−9.3
	3	3	18.5	16.9	1.2	−12.5	−24.2	−27.4	−26.9	−22.7	−11.0
		6	23.2	20.2	10.8	4.0	−4.4	−11.6	−16.6	−18.0	−10.4
		9	18.7	14.7	9.3	6.4	1.5	−4.7	−10.7	−14.5	−9.9
	5	3	31.6	30.7	−11.1	−36.1	−53.1	−47.9	−37.5	−26.8	−11.4
		6	41.4	34.9	12.1	−0.4	−13.7	−20.5	−22.8	−21.0	−10.8
		9	33.0	23.9	11.6	6.3	−1.4	−8.8	−14.4	−16.7	−10.2

Parents Pay

g	h_t	r	Born in 2015	Future genera-tions	0	10	20	30	40	50	60
1.25	0	3	4.5	3.9	4.1	4.9	4.6	-5.0	-13.5	-17.3	-10.4
		6	3.8	3.8	3.7	5.7	7.7	0.5	-7.9	-13.8	-9.8
		9	2.1	2.1	2.1	4.2	7.4	2.5	-4.7	-11.2	-9.3
	3	3	12.7	10.7	5.8	-0.6	-8.1	-18.9	-23.4	-22.1	-11.0
		6	10.9	10.2	7.7	7.5	5.4	-5.2	-13.6	-17.4	-10.4
		9	6.1	5.5	4.5	6.5	7.9	0.3	-8.1	-13.9	-9.9
	5	3	25.3	20.8	5.6	-13.1	-30.3	-37.5	-33.6	-26.1	-11.4
		6	21.7	19.5	12.3	7.8	-0.1	-12.9	-19.5	-20.3	-10.8
		9	12.0	10.4	7.4	8.4	7.2	-2.9	-11.5	-16.2	-10.2

NOTE: r = discount rate; g = productivity growth rate; h_t = rate of growth in health care outlay per person relative to earnings.
SOURCE: Authors.

49

Notes

1. Mark Hall, *Reforming Private Health Insurance* (Washington, D.C.: AEI Press, 1994), pp. 38–40.

2. Health Security Act, H.R. 3600, 103d Cong., 2nd sess. (1994).

3. "Community-rated Health Plans Prove Popular, but Success May Depend on Universal Coverage," *Wall Street Journal,* June 15, 1994.

4. Remarks by President Bill Clinton to the Conference of Business for Social Responsibility, Grand Hyatt Hotel, Washington, D.C., October 21, 1993.

5. Laurence J. Kotlikoff, *Generational Accounting: Knowing Who Pays, and When, for What We Spend* (New York: Free Press, 1992); and Alan Auerbach, Jagadeesh Gokhale, and Laurence Kotlikoff, "Generational Accounts: A Meaningful Alternative to Deficit Accounting," in David F. Bradford, ed., *Tax Policy and the Economy,* vol. 5 (Cambridge: MIT Press, 1991), pp. 55–110.

6. Office of Management and Budget, *Budget of the United States Government, Analytical Perspectives, Fiscal Year 1995,* February 1994, pp. 21–31.

7. Employee Benefits Research Institute, *Health Reform: Examining the Alternatives,* Issue brief 147, March 1994, pp. 21–22.

8. Phyllis A. Doran, Alice F. Rosenblatt, and Dale H. Yamamoto, *A Review of Premium Estimates in the Health Security Act,* Monograph seven, American Academy of Actuaries, April 1994, p. ii.

9. The "expected alliance population" refers to the average insurance pool expected under the HSA. Because it is randomly formed, and representative, we use this estimate as the expected average premium for the entire population.

10. Council of Economic Advisers, *Economic Report of the President and Annual Report of the Council of Economic Advisers* (Wash-

ington, D.C.: U.S. Government Printing Office, January 1993); Congressional Budget Office, *Trends in Health Spending: An Update,* June 1993; and Sally T. Burner, Daniel R. Waldo, and David R. McKusick, "National Health Expenditures Projections through 2030," *Health Care Financing Review* (Fall 1992), pp. 2–29.

11. See also Victor R. Fuchs, "The Health Sector's Share of the Gross National Product," *Science,* vol. 247, Feb. 2, 1990.

12. CEA, *Consumer Expenditure Survey,* p. 162; CBO, *Trends in Health Spending;* and Burner, Waldo, and McKusick, "National Health Expenditures Projections."

13. William J. Baumol, "Health Care, Education and the Cost Disease: A Looming Crisis for Public Choice," *Public Choice,* vol. 77 (1993), pp. 17–28; and David F. Bradford, "Balance on Unbalanced Growth," *Zeitschrift für Nationalökonomie* (1969), pp. 291–304.

14. For a discussion, see Council of Economic Advisers, *Economic Report of the President,* 1993, chap. 4.

15. American Academy of Actuaries, *Health Risk Assessment and Health Risk Adjustment—Crucial Elements in Effective Health Care Reform,* May 1993, pp. 3–4.

16. There is some controversy as to the effectiveness of risk adjustment models to predict expected loss. See, for example, Joseph P. Newhouse, "Patients at Risk: Health Reform and Risk Adjustment," *Health Affairs,* (Spring (I) 1994). While Newhouse does question the accuracy of different adjusters, he concludes that even a small increase in predictive ability can lead to large returns.

17. See D. Lefkowitz and A. Monheit, "Health Insurance, Use of Health Services, and Health Care Expenditures," *National Medical Expenditure Survey Research Findings 12,* Agency for Health Care Policy and Research, December 1991; and Daniel R. Waldo, Sally T. Sonnefeld, David R. McKusick, and Ross R. Arnett III, "Health Expenditures by Age Group, 1977 and 1987," *Health Care Financing Review* (Summer 1989), pp. 111–20.

18. Data are from projections of the Social Security Administration, provided by Jagadeesh Gokhale.

19. Jennifer Cheeseman Day, "Population Projections of the United States, by Age, Sex, Race and Hispanic Origin: 1993–2050," P25-1104, U.S. Bureau of the Census, Washington, D.C.: U.S. Government Printing Office, 1993.

20. These results are in line with other estimates of the transfers by age. See, for example, Committee for a Responsible Federal Budget, "Community Rating and Cross Subsidies under the Health Security Act," June 30, 1994.

21. Hall, *Reforming Private Health Insurance.*

22. Sherry Glied, *Revising the Tax Treatment of Employer-provided Health Insurance* (Washington, D.C.: AEI Press, 1994).

23. Louise Sheiner, "Health Care Costs, Wages, and Aging: Assessing the Impact of Community Rating," Ms., Federal Reserve Board of Governors, December 1994.

24. The data on natality originate from *Vital Statistics of the United States, 1990,* vol. 1: *Natality* (Hyattsville, Md.: U.S. Department of Health and Human Services, 1994), p. 103. The data are arranged to depict total live births in 1990 per each age of mother, ten to forty-seven. For simplicity, the insignificant extremes were ignored.

About the Authors

DAVID F. BRADFORD is professor of economics and public affairs at the Woodrow Wilson School of Public and International Affairs, Princeton University, and adjunct professor of law at New York University. He is an adjunct scholar of the American Enterprise Institute and a research associate of the National Bureau of Economic Advisers. Mr. Bradford was a member of the President's Council of Economic Advisers from 1991 to 1993 and was the deputy assistant secretary for tax policy at the Treasury Department from 1975 to 1977. He is the author of several publications on tax policy, including (together with the U.S. Treasury Tax Policy Staff) *Blueprints for Basic Tax Reform* (second edition, 1984) and *Untangling the Income Tax* (1986). He is editor of *Distributional Analysis of Tax Policy* (AEI Press, 1995).

DERRICK A. MAX is a professional staff economist for the Committee on Economic and Educational Opportunities of the U.S. House of Representatives and was a research assistant at the American Enterprise Institute.

Board of Trustees

Wilson H. Taylor, *Chairman*
Chairman and CEO
CIGNA Corporation

Tully M. Friedman, *Treasurer*
Hellman & Friedman

Edwin L. Artzt
Chairman of the Executive Committee
The Procter & Gamble
  Company

Joseph A. Cannon
Chairman and CEO
Geneva Steel Company

Dick Cheney
Chairman, President, and CEO
Halliburton Company

Albert J. Costello
President and CEO
W. R. Grace & Co.

Harlan Crow
Managing Partner
Crow Family Holdings

Christopher C. DeMuth
President
American Enterprise Institute

Malcolm S. Forbes, Jr.
President and CEO
Forbes Inc.

Christopher B. Galvin
President and COO
Motorola, Inc.

Harvey Golub
Chairman and CEO
American Express Company

Robert F. Greenhill
Chairman
Greenhill & Co. LLC

M. Douglas Ivester
President and COO
The Coca-Cola Company

Martin M. Koffel
Chairman and CEO
URS Corporation

Bruce Kovner
Chairman
Caxton Corporation

Kenneth L. Lay
Chairman and CEO
ENRON Corp.

The American Enterprise Institute for Public Policy Research

Founded in 1943, AEI is a nonpartisan, nonprofit, research and educational organization based in Washington, D.C. The Institute sponsors research, conducts seminars and conferences, and publishes books and periodicals.

AEI's research is carried out under three major programs: Economic Policy Studies; Foreign Policy and Defense Studies; and Social and Political Studies. The resident scholars and fellows listed in these pages are part of a network that also includes ninety adjunct scholars at leading universities throughout the United States and in several foreign countries.

The views expressed in AEI publications are those of the authors and do not necessarily reflect the views of the staff, advisory panels, officers, or trustees.

Marilyn Ware Lewis
Chairman
American Water Works Company, Inc.

Alex J. Mandl
President and COO
AT&T

Craig O. McCaw
Chairman and CEO
Eagle River, Inc.

Paul H. O'Neill
Chairman and CEO
Aluminum Company of America

George R. Roberts
Kohlberg Kravis Roberts & Co.

John W. Rowe
President and CEO
New England Electric System

Edward B. Rust, Jr.
President and CEO
State Farm Insurance Companies

James P. Schadt
Chairman and CEO
Reader's Digest Association, Inc.

John W. Snow
Chairman, President, and CEO
CSX Corporation

William S. Stavropoulos
President and CEO
The Dow Chemical Company

James Q. Wilson
James A. Collins Professor
  of Management
University of California
  at Los Angeles

Officers

Christopher C. DeMuth
President

David B. Gerson
Executive Vice President

Council of Academic Advisers

James Q. Wilson, *Chairman*
James A. Collins Professor
  of Management
University of California
  at Los Angeles

Gertrude Himmelfarb
Distinguished Professor of History
  Emeritus
City University of New York

Samuel P. Huntington
Eaton Professor of the
  Science of Government
Harvard University

D. Gale Johnson
Eliakim Hastings Moore
  Distinguished Service Professor
  of Economics Emeritus
University of Chicago

illiam M. Landes
fton R. Musser Professor of
  conomics
 iversity of Chicago Law School

m Peltzman
 ars Roebuck Professor of Economics
 nd Financial Services
 iversity of Chicago
 raduate School of Business

 lson W. Polsby
 ofessor of Political Science
 iversity of California at Berkeley

 orge L. Priest
 in M. Olin Professor of Law and
  conomics
  le Law School

 urray L. Weidenbaum
 allinckrodt Distinguished
 University Professor
 ashington University

esearch Staff

 on Aron
 sident Scholar

 aude E. Barfield
 sident Scholar; Director, Science
 and Technology Policy Studies

 nthia A. Beltz
 search Fellow

 alter Berns
 sident Scholar

 ouglas J. Besharov
 sident Scholar

 obert H. Bork
 in M. Olin Scholar in Legal Studies

 arlyn Bowman
 sident Fellow

 hn E. Calfee
 sident Scholar

 nne V. Cheney
 . H. Brady, Jr., Distinguished Fellow

 nesh D'Souza
 in M. Olin Research Fellow

 cholas N. Eberstadt
 siting Scholar

Mark Falcoff
Resident Scholar

John D. Fonte
Visiting Scholar

Gerald R. Ford
Distinguished Fellow

Murray F. Foss
Visiting Scholar

Diana Furchtgott-Roth
Assistant to the President and Resident
  Fellow

Suzanne Garment
Resident Scholar

Jeffrey Gedmin
Research Fellow

Patrick Glynn
Resident Scholar

Robert A. Goldwin
Resident Scholar

Robert W. Hahn
Resident Scholar

Thomas Hazlett
Visiting Scholar

Robert B. Helms
Resident Scholar; Director, Health
  Policy Studies

Glenn Hubbard
Visiting Scholar

Douglas Irwin
Henry Wendt Scholar in Political
  Economy

James D. Johnston
Resident Fellow

Jeane J. Kirkpatrick
Senior Fellow; Director, Foreign and
  Defense Policy Studies

Marvin H. Kosters
Resident Scholar; Director,
  Economic Policy Studies

Irving Kristol
John M. Olin Distinguished Fellow

Dana Lane
Director of Publications

Michael A. Ledeen
Resident Scholar

James Lilley
Resident Fellow; Director, Asian
  Studies Program

John H. Makin
Resident Scholar; Director, Fiscal
  Policy Studies

Allan H. Meltzer
Visiting Scholar

Joshua Muravchik
Resident Scholar

Charles Murray
Bradley Fellow

Michael Novak
George F. Jewett Scholar in Religion,
  Philosophy, and Public Policy;
  Director, Social and
  Political Studies

Norman J. Ornstein
Resident Scholar

Richard N. Perle
Resident Fellow

William Schneider
Resident Scholar

William Shew
Visiting Scholar

J. Gregory Sidak
F. K. Weyerhaeuser Fellow

Herbert Stein
Senior Fellow

Irwin M. Stelzer
Resident Scholar; Director, Regulatory
  Policy Studies

W. Allen Wallis
Resident Scholar

Ben J. Wattenberg
Senior Fellow

Carolyn L. Weaver
Resident Scholar; Director, Social
  Security and Pension Studies

www.ingramcontent.com/pod-product-compliance
Lightning Source LLC
Jackson TN
JSHW061756151224
75386JS00041BA/1530